Contents

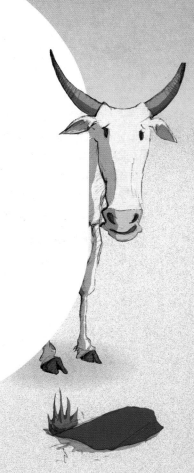

OXFORD
UNIVERSITY PRESS

Great Clarendon Street, Oxford, OX2 6DP, United Kingdom

Oxford University Press is a department of the University
of Oxford. It furthers the University's objective of excellence
in research, scholarship, and education by publishing
worldwide. Oxford is a registered trade mark of Oxford
University Press in the UK and in certain other countries

Text © Julia Donaldson 2009
Illustrations © Oxford University Press 2009

The moral rights of the author have been asserted

This edition first published 2018

British Library Cataloguing in Publication Data
Data available

ISBN: 978-0-19-276478-2

10 9 8 7 6 5 4 3 2 1

Paper used in the production of this book is a natural, recyclable product
made from wood grown in sustainable forests. The manufacturing process
conforms to the environmental regulations of the country of origin.

Printed in China

Acknowledgements

Series Editor: Clare Kirtley

Cover illustration by Jonathan Allen

The Ox and the Yak illustrated by Thomas Docherty

The Doll in the Bin illustrated by Joelle Dreidemy

Animal Quiz illustrated by Carol Liddiment

The Seven Kids illustrated by Andy Hammond

Ron Rabbit's Egg illustrated by Jonathan Allen

The Big Match illustrated by Chris Mould

The Shopping List illustrated by Anni Axworthy

The Ox and the Yak

Tips for reading The Ox and the Yak together

This story practises these letter patterns:

ch th ng ck x qu

Ask your child to point to these letter patterns and say the sounds (e.g. *x* as in *fox*). Look out for these letter patterns in the story.

Your child might find these words tricky:

the of was he said good
one very so some two

These words are common, but your child may not have learned how to sound them out yet. Say the words for your child if they do not know them.

Before you begin, ask your child to read the title by sounding out first (say each letter out loud, e.g. *y-a-k*) and then blending the word together (e.g. *yak*) as much as possible. Look at the picture together. What do you think this story is about?

Remind your child to read unfamiliar words by saying the individual sounds and then blending them together quickly to read the word. When you have finished reading the story, look through it again and:

- Talk about what's in the man's box. Ask your child, *Does it contain good luck? Why?*

- Find the words that rhyme on pages 18-19 (*quack, back*). Try to write the word *quack*. Say all the sounds in the word (*qu-a-ck*) then write the letter patterns that make each sound.

On the back of an ox
sat a man with a box

and in the man's box
was a bag of odd socks.

On the back of a yak
sat a man with a pack
and in the man's pack
was a duck with a quack.

The man on the ox
met the man with the duck
and he said, "In this box
is a bag of good luck."

The men had a chat
and the duck got a hat.

It was one of the socks
from the bag in the box.

Then the man on the ox
sang a very long song
and the man on the yak
hit a very big gong.

The yak did a jig
and so did the ox
and the duck had some fun
with the bag of odd socks.

Then the duck said,
"Quack quack!"
and the two men went back

on the back of the ox
and the back of the yak.

The Doll in the Bin

Tips for reading The Doll in the Bin together

This story practises these letter patterns:

ll   ss   ff   sh   th   wh   ng   ck   x

Ask your child to point to these letter patterns and say the sounds (e.g. *ff* as in *cuff*). Look out for these letter patterns in the story.

Your child might find these words tricky:

he   her   the   to   of   she   are   have
come   says   school   gives   wash   let's

These words are common, but your child may not have learned how to sound them out yet. Say the words for your child if they do not know them.

Before you begin, ask your child to read the title by sounding out first (say each sound out loud, e.g. *d-o-ll*) and then blending the word together (e.g. *doll*) as much as possible. Look at the picture together. What do you think this story is about?

Remind your child to read unfamiliar words by saying the individual sounds and then blending them together quickly to read the word. When you have finished reading the story, look through it again and:

- Ask your child, *Have you ever lost something? How did you feel?*

- Find the words that end with the letter pattern *th* (*Beth, with*). Try to write the word *with*. Say all the sounds in the word (e.g. *w-i-th*) then write the letter patterns that make each sound.

This is Beth and this is Jill.
Jill is Beth's doll.

This is Puff. Puff is Beth's cat.
When Beth is in bed,
Puff gets Jill.

Puff is patting Jill.
He pats her into the bin!

The bin men have come to get the rubbish.

The men tip the bins into
the back of a big van.
Jill is in this bin bag!

Beth is sad.

She is missing Jill.

The bin men tip the rubbish into
a big pit.

Lots of things are in the pit.
Pots, tubs, boxes . . . and Jill!

This is Tess. Tess is at the rubbish tip with her mum.

"Mum!" says Tess. "Is that a doll in the pit?"

A man picks up the doll.
He gives her to Mum.

Tess is in school. "This doll fell in a pit," she says.

"That's Jill!" says Beth.

Tess gives Jill back to Beth.

Beth gives Tess a set of peg dolls.

Animal Quiz

Tips for reading Animal Quiz together

This story practises these letter patterns:

ll   zz   sh   ch   th   ff   wh   ng
ck   x   qu

Ask your child to point to these letter patterns and say the sounds (e.g. *zz* as in *buzz*). Look out for these letter patterns in the story.

Your child might find these words tricky:

the   of   have   she   she's   their
or   they   do   give   to   into

These words are common, but your child may not have learned how to sound them out yet. Say the words for your child if they do not know them.

Before you begin, ask your child to read the title by sounding out first (say each sound out loud, e.g. *qu-i-z*) and then blending the word together (e.g. *quiz*) as much as possible. Look at the picture together. What do you think this story is about?

Remind your child to read unfamiliar words by saying the individual sounds and then blending them together quickly to read the word. When you have finished reading the story, look through it again and:

- Talk about the animal homes shown on pages 45-48 (a nest and a den). Ask your child, *Which animals live in these homes?*
- Find the words that contain the letter patterns *wh* and *ch* (*which, chips, chicks*). Try to write the word *which*. Say all the sounds in the word (*wh-i-ch*) then write the letter patterns that make each sound.

This is the tip of a wing.
Is it a robin, a duck or a bat?

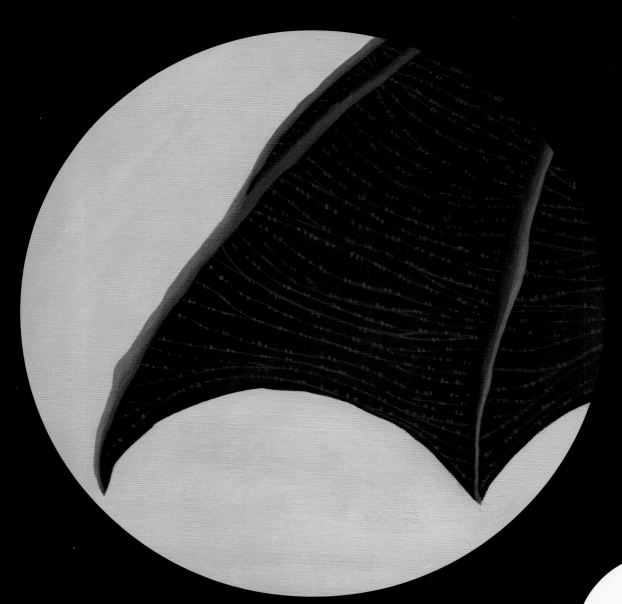

It's a bat!

Which animal's leg is this?
Is it an ox, a camel or a rat?

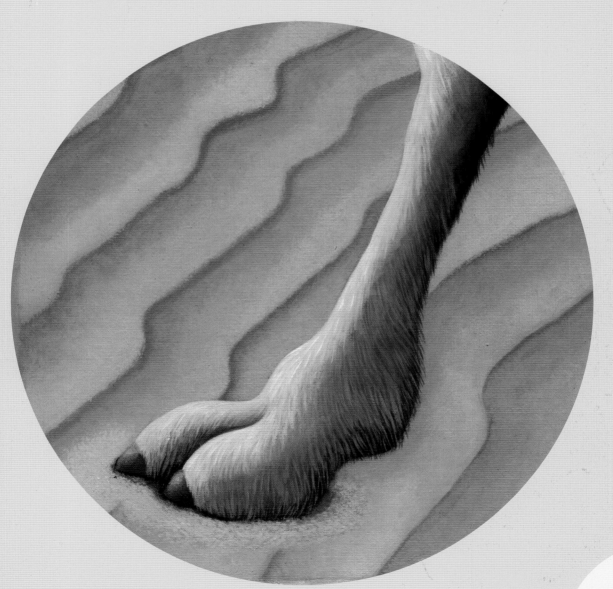

It's a camel! Camels have long legs.

The chicks have a mum.
Is she a gull, a hen or a puffin?

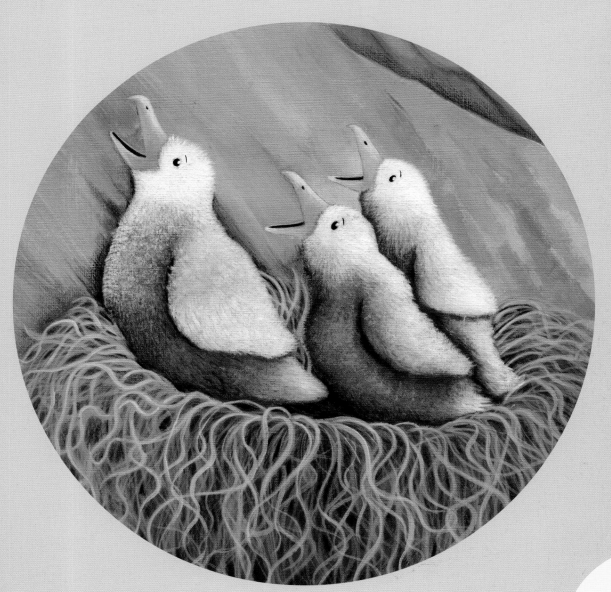

Yes, she's a gull.

Fox cubs in a den. Is their mum a yak, an ox or a vixen?

Yes! Their mum is a vixen.

This is a robin. Will it quack, sing or buzz?

Robins sing. They do not quack or buzz.

This animal is in its mum's pocket.
Is it a cat, a wombat or a bat?

It's a wombat.

Which dish will Mick give to his rabbit? A dish of carrots, jam or chips?

Carrots – not chips or jam!

Seven eggs. Will they hatch into chickens, ducklings or parrots?

Tap, tap, tap! Seven ducklings!

The Seven Kids

Tips for reading The Seven Kids together

This story practises these letter patterns:

ll ff sh th ck x qu

Ask your child to point to these letter patterns and say the sounds (e.g. *sh* as in *shut*). Look out for these letter patterns in the story.

Your child might find these words tricky:

**live the do me we no
puts what**

These words are common, but your child may not have learned how to sound them out yet. Say the words for your child if they do not know them.

Before you begin, ask your child to read the title by sounding out first (say each letter out loud, e.g. *k-i-d-s*) and then blending the word together (e.g. *kids*) as much as possible. Look at the picture together. What do you think this story is about?

Remind your child to read unfamiliar words by saying the individual sounds and then blending them together quickly to read the word. When you have finished reading the story, look through it again and:

- Talk about how the fox feels at the end of the story.
- Find the words that begin with the letter pattern *sh* (*shack, shop, shall*). Think of some words that end with the letter pattern *sh* (*fish, dish, wish*). Make up a rhyme using your words (e.g. *a fish on a dish as you wish*).

Seven kids live in a shack
with Mum.

Mum tells the kids, "Do not let the fox in."

Mum is at the shop.

63

65

But it is not Mum. It is the fox, with a big sack.

The fox puts six kids in his sack.
But Ken kid is in a box.

The fox sets off with his sack.
Ken kid runs.

The fox has a nap. Ken runs to the shop.

Mum and Ken cut the sack.

The six kids run back to
the shack.

Mum and Ken put six rocks in the sack.

The fox is in his den.

But what is this?

Ron Rabbit's Egg

Tips for reading Ron Rabbit's Egg together

This story practises these letter patterns:

ll zz sh ch tch th wh ng ck x

Ask your child to point to these letter patterns and say the sounds (e.g. *tch* as in *hatch*). Look out for these letter patterns in the story.

Your child might find these words tricky:

out of he says give me I the make have play be

These words are common, but your child may not have learned how to sound them out yet. Say the words for your child if they do not know them.

Before you begin, ask your child to read the title by sounding out first (say each letter out loud, e.g. *R-o-n*) and then blending the word together (e.g. *Ron*) as much as possible. Look at the picture together. What do you think this story is about?

Remind your child to read unfamiliar words by saying the individual sounds and then blending them together quickly to read the word. When you have finished reading the story, look through it again and:

- Ask your child, *What would you do with the egg?*
- Find some words that end with the *ch* sound (*hatch, catch, rich, such*). Notice the sound *ch* is spelled two different ways. Try to write the word *catch*. Say all the sounds in the word (e.g. *c-a-tch*) then write the letter patterns that make each sound.

Ron Rabbit has an egg.
"A chicken will hatch out
of this egg," he says.

"Then, when that chicken is a hen, it will give me lots of eggs.

If I sell the eggs, I can get a big pot.

Then I can make lots of jam.

If I sell the jam, I can get a fishing rod.

I will catch lots of fish and sell them.

Then I will be rich! I can have lots of things.

I can have a hammock and
a big box of chocs.

I can have a chess set.

I can have a tennis racket.

I can play jazz on a sax.

I can have a jacket with lots of pockets and zips and buttons,

and thick mittens, and a hat with a pompom.

I will be in the jet set!"

But then ... bang!

"That egg had such a thin shell!"
says Ron Rabbit.

The Big Match

Tips for reading The Big Match together

This story practises these letter patterns:

ng   ck   x   qu

Ask your child to point to these letter patterns and say the sounds (e.g. *x* as in *fox*, not the letter name *ex*). Look out for these letter patterns in the story.

Your child might find these words tricky:

ball   begun   come   here
match   the

These words are common, but your child may not have learned how to sound them out yet. Say the words for your child if they do not know them.

Before you begin, ask your child to read the title by sounding out first (say each letter out loud, e.g. *b-i-g*) and then blending the word together (e.g. *big*) as much as possible. Look at the picture together. What do you think this story is about?

Remind your child to read unfamiliar words by saying the individual sounds separately and then blending them together quickly to read the word. When you have finished reading, look through the story again and:

- Talk about why Max Fox got sent off. Ask your child, *How do you think the ducks felt at the end of the story?*

- Find the words which end with the letter pattern *ck* (*duck, quack, kick, Rick*). Say the sound that these two letters make at the end of words. Can you find some words that end with the letter pattern *x*? (*six, fox, Max*).

Here come the fans.

Here come the six ducks.

Here come the six foxes.

The duck fans quack.

The fox fans sing.

The ref rings a bell. The match has begun!

The foxes and ducks kick the ball.

Rick Duck gets the ball in.

Max Fox gets the ball in.

Yes!

The ducks get the ball.

Max Fox kicks Rick Duck!

The duck fans quack.

The ref rings his bell.

Get off, Max!

Rick Duck gets the ball in!

The duck fans quack and sing.

The ducks win the match.

The Shopping List

Tips for reading The Shopping List together

This story practises blending groups of consonants at the end of words. Look out for these in the story:

we**nt**   ba**nk**   he**ld**   li**st**   li**ft**
go**lf**   la**mp**   mi**lk**

Your child might find these words tricky:

ball   home   I   like   the   they   to

These words are common, but your child may not have learned how to sound them out yet. Say the words for your child if they do not know them.

Before you begin, ask your child to read the title by sounding out first (say each sound out loud, e.g. *l-i-st*) and then blending the word together (e.g. *list*) as much as possible. Look at the picture together. What do you think this story is about?

Remind your child to read unfamiliar words by saying the individual sounds separately and then blending them together quickly to read the word. When you have finished reading, look through the story again and:

- Talk about why Yasmin and Dad ended up with the wrong shopping. Ask your child, *What do you think they should do now?*

- Encourage your child to find two words in the story that rhyme (*vest, best; got, lot; back, unpack*). Notice that only the first letter is different. Can you think of any other words that rhyme with *best*? (*nest, test, west*)

Yasmin and Dad went to the bank.

Next, they went shopping.

Yasmin held the shopping list.

belt
golf ball
lamp

Yasmin and Dad went to a big shop. They got in the lift.

A man got in with them.

120

Yasmin and Dad got back in
the lift.

The man got in with them.

Yasmin and Dad went back home.